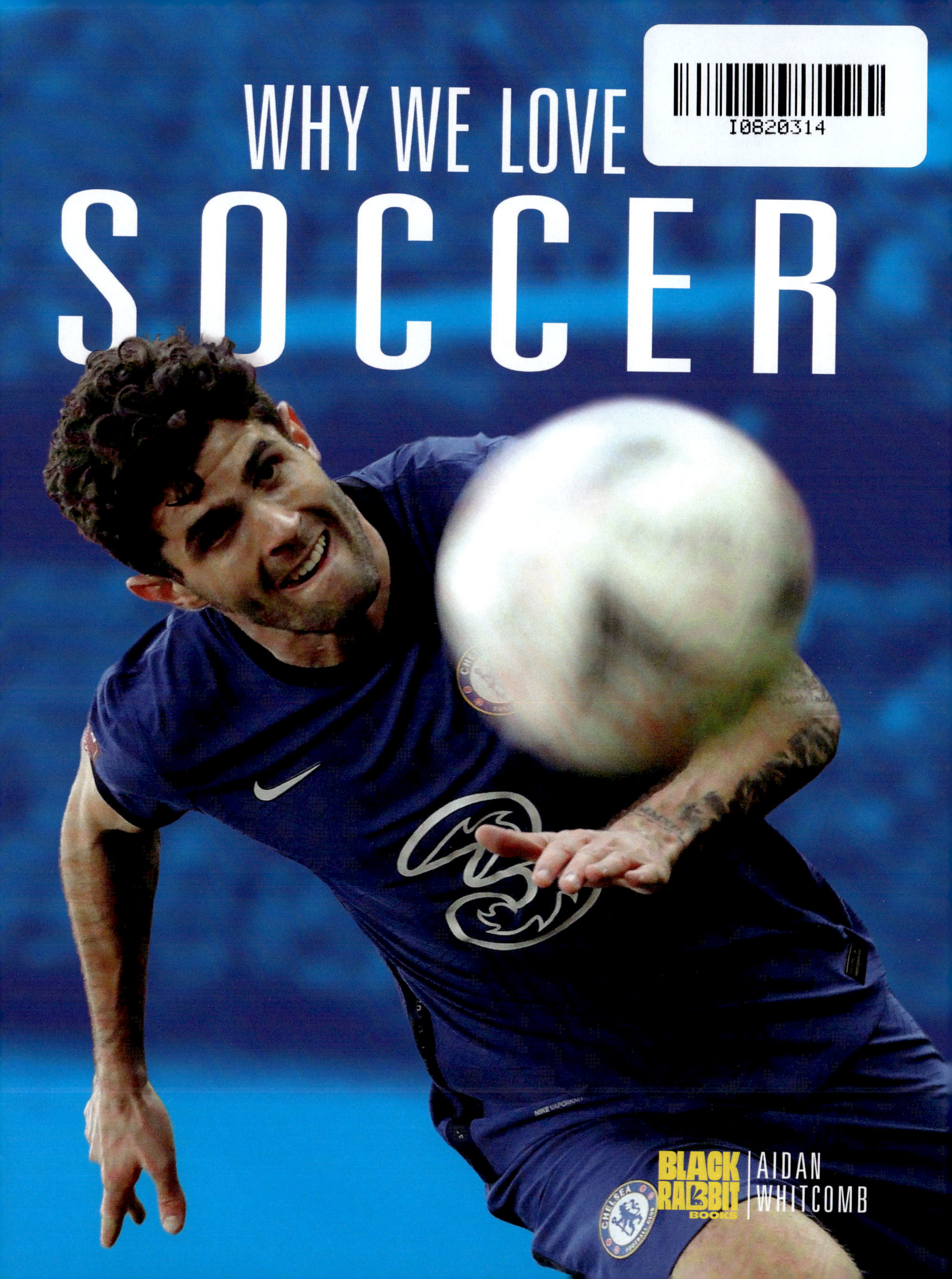
WHY WE LOVE
SOCCER
BLACK RABBIT BOOKS
AIDAN WHITCOMB

TABLE OF CONTENTS

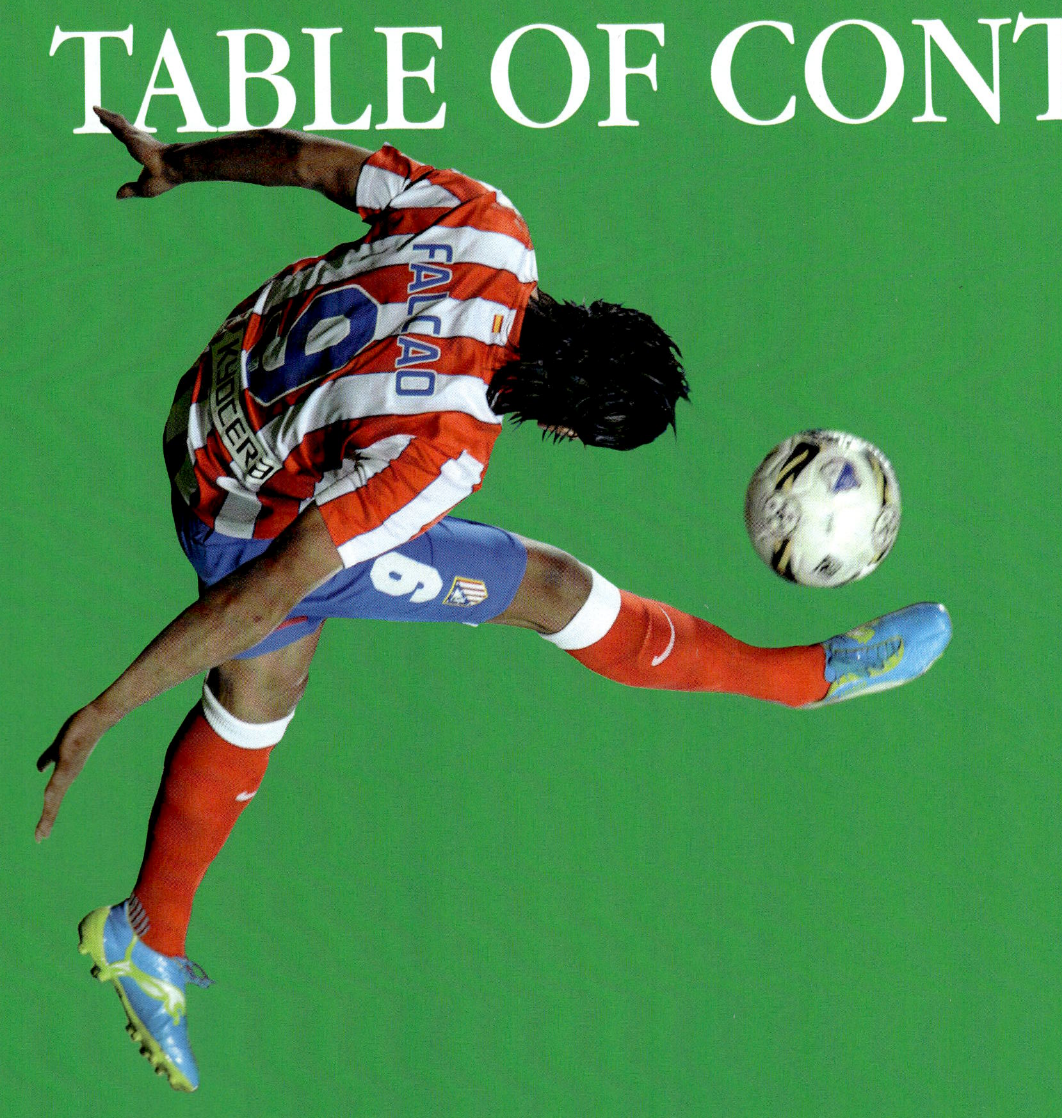

1

Soccer's Start

Soccer is an old sport. It started in England in 1863. The game spread around the world. It is called football outside the United States. In 1904, the International Federation of Association Football (FIFA) was created. FIFA organizes soccer worldwide.

Soccer is most popular in Europe and South America. Fans love soccer there. The sport is growing in the United States. There are men's and women's leagues. Both have incredible players. Fans love watching them score!

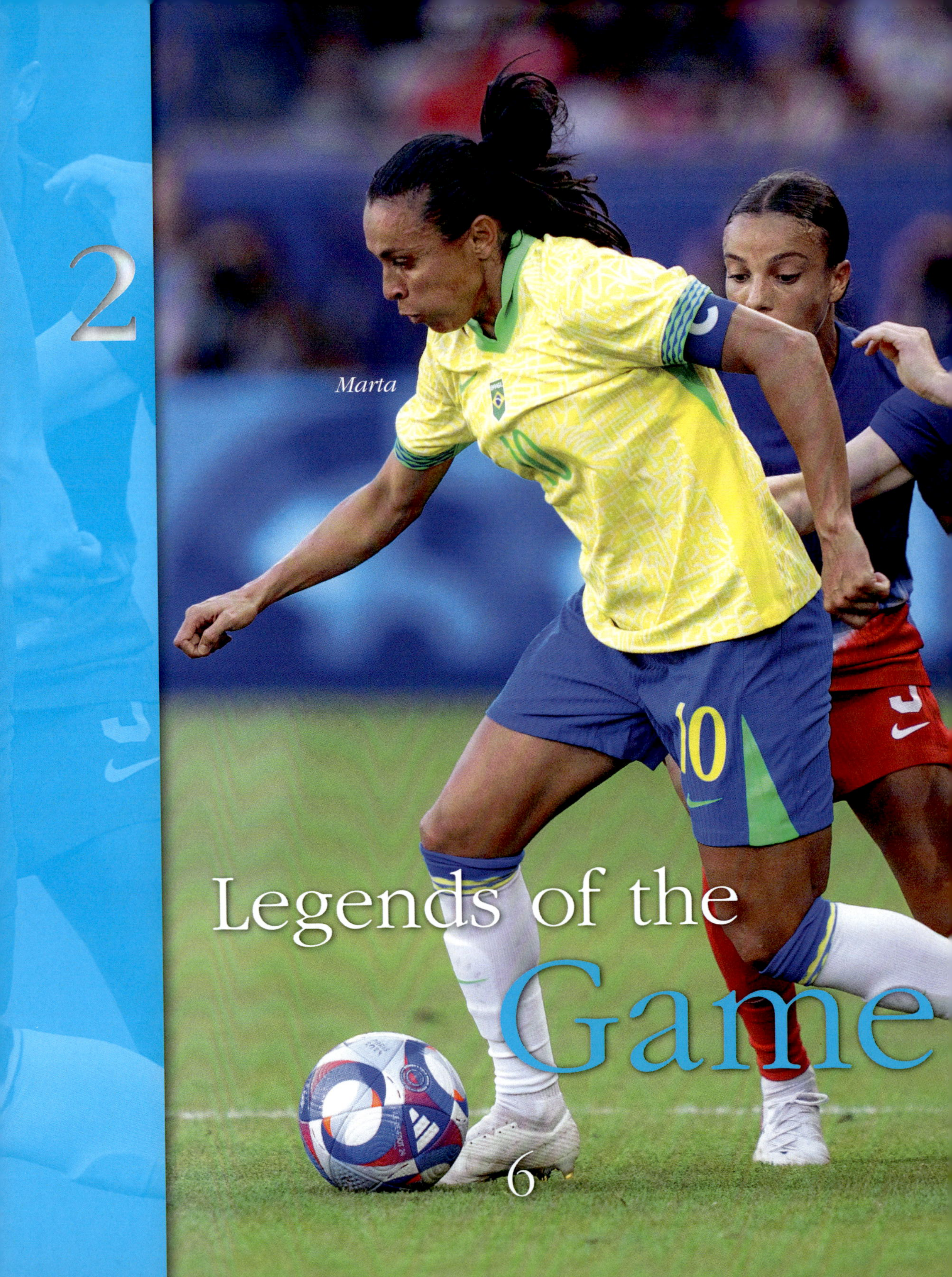

2

Marta

Legends of the Game

Soccer has many legends. Marta is often considered the greatest women's player. She was the first player to score in five World Cups! Others think Mia Hamm is the best. Hamm won two World Cups. She also has two Olympic gold medals.

In men's soccer, fans love Lionel Messi and Cristiano Ronaldo. Fans debate which is the GOAT. Messi has won the most team trophies ever. Ronaldo is the top scorer of all time. He has more than 900 goals!

Lionel Messi

Think About It
Who is soccer's GOAT? What skills make them the best?

3

The Fan Experience

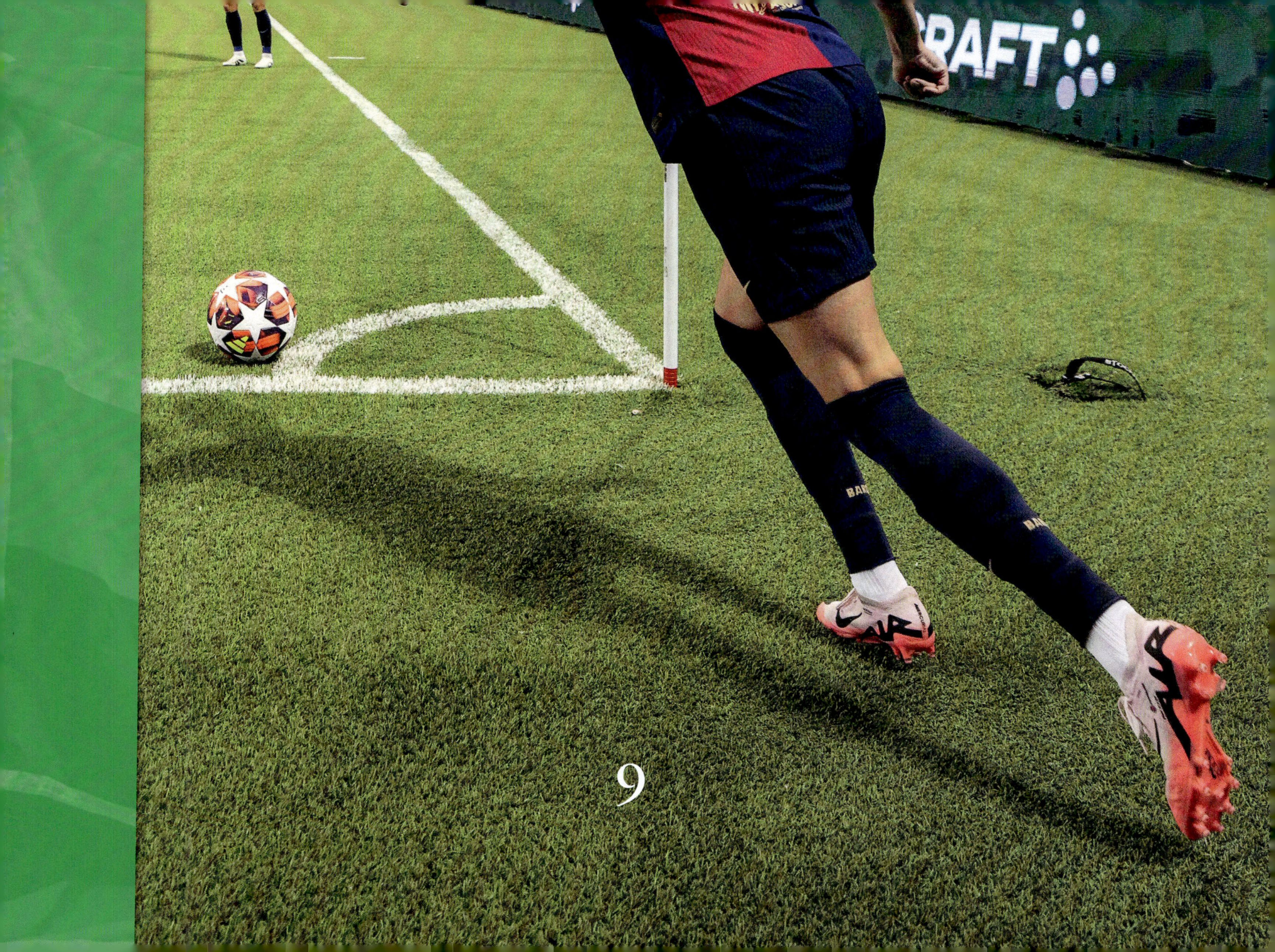

Soccer fans have great pride in their teams. They are very loud. Some fans are called ultras. They bring flags and drums. They chant and sing all game long.

The biggest teams have fans worldwide. **Club teams** like Real Madrid and Barcelona are huge. They have millions of fans. People around the world watch their games on TV. **National teams** also have many fans. People love to root for their country.

Did You Know?
The World Cup takes place every four years.

Madridista
Real Madrid

4

The Global Game

Soccer is the most popular sport in the world. Nearly every country has a league. Some have multiple leagues. By far, Mexico has the most pro teams. It had 244 teams in 2023! Fans have many clubs to root for.

England has the most-watched soccer league. The Premier League has 20 clubs. These clubs have millions of fans. Teams like Liverpool and Manchester United are very famous. They have long histories.

Women's Champion League match

Did You Know?
Europe's best teams play in a special **tournament**. It is called the Champions League.

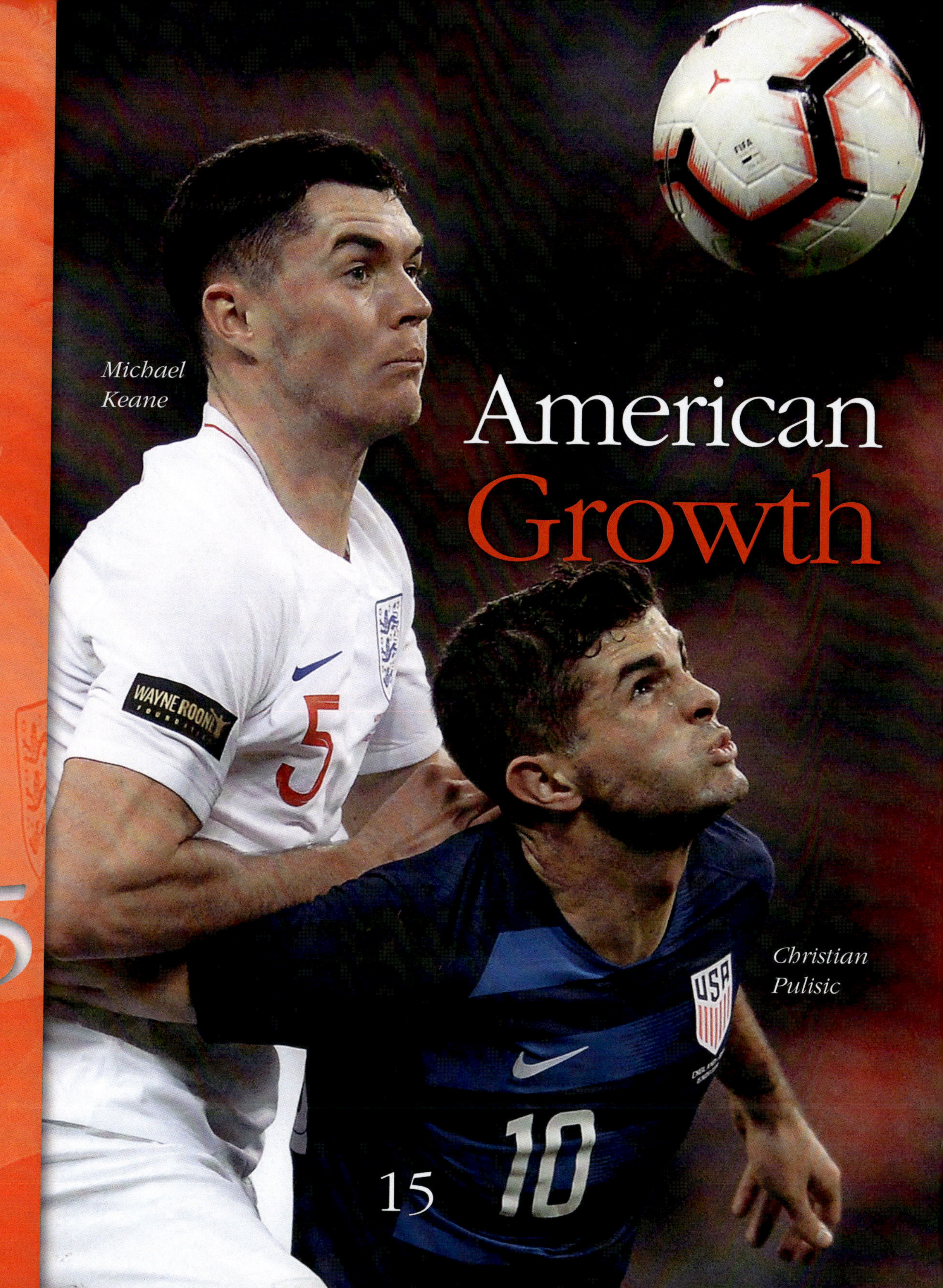

Michael Keane

American Growth

Christian Pulisic

Soccer had a late start in the United States. Baseball, basketball, and football are more popular. But soccer is gaining more US fans. It is one of the fastest growing team sports in the country. Clubs like LA Galaxy and Inter Miami have a lot of fans.

American superstars help grow the game. Christian Pulisic and Trinity Rodman are two stars. They both are great scorers and dribblers. Fans from other sports are tuning in.

Famous English player David Beckham use to played on the LA Galaxy.

Think About It
Who do you think is the best US player ever?

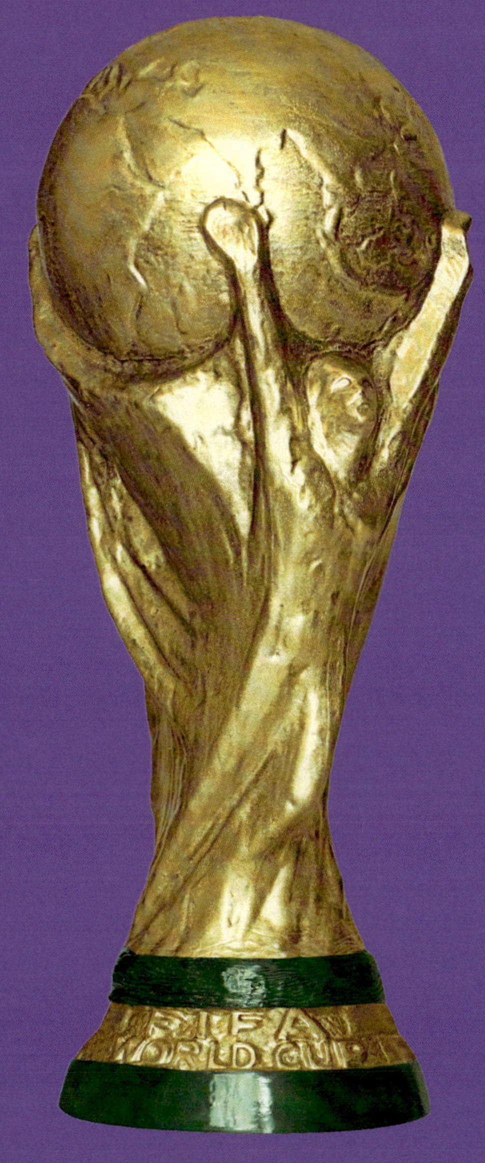

The World Cup

6

The World Cup is the biggest sporting event in the world. It happens every four years. Many national teams compete. It attracts many viewers. In 2022, about 5 billion people watched!

In 2026, the World Cup will come to North America. Cities across the continent will host games. It will be an exciting time for soccer fans!

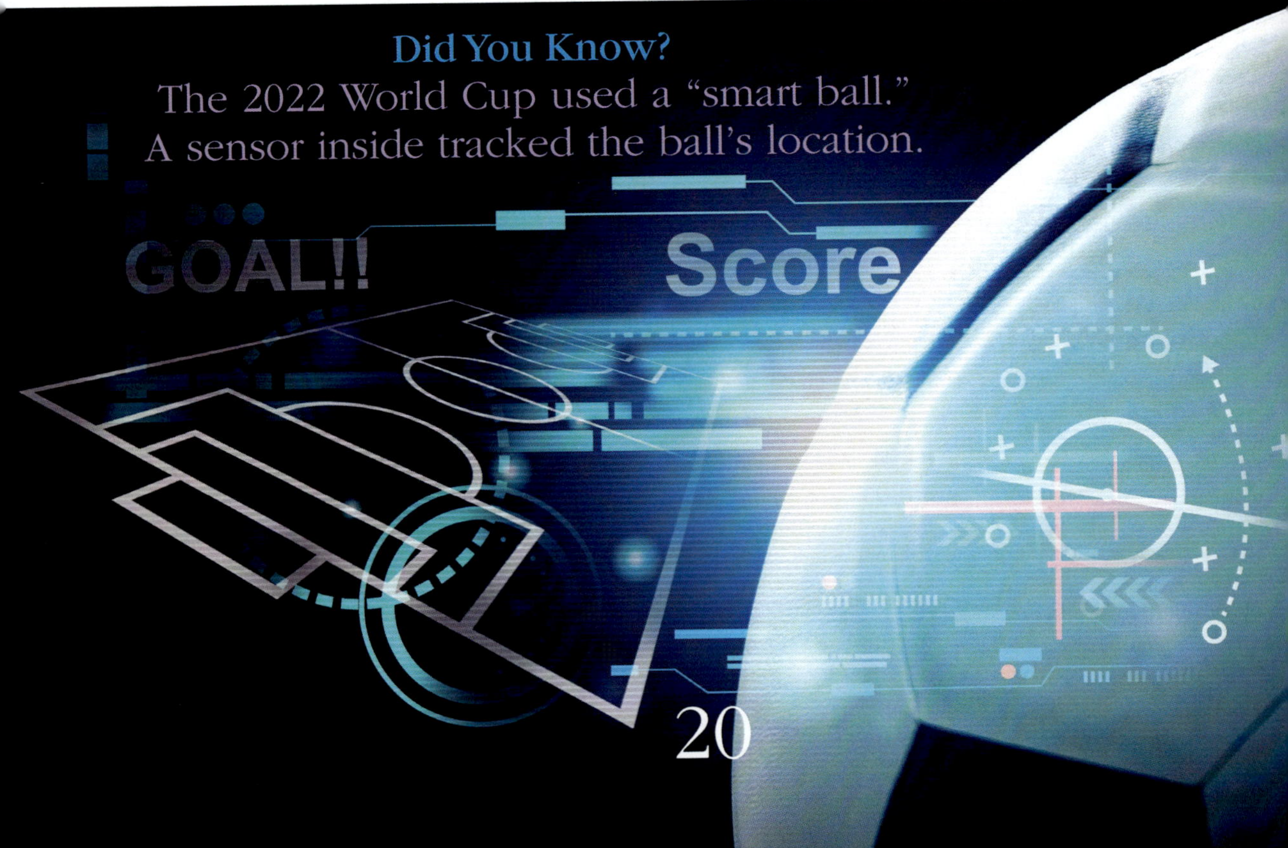

Did You Know?
The 2022 World Cup used a "smart ball." A sensor inside tracked the ball's location.

21

MORE TO EXPLORE

FANTASTIC FACTS

Club team Paris Saint-Germain signed Neymar for a record $263 million in 2017.

Elena Danilova is the youngest player ever to score at a World Cup. She was just 16!

Marta has scored 17 career World Cup goals. That is the most in men's or women's history.

Goalkeeper Tom King scored a 105-yard (96-meter) goal in 2021. It is the farthest ever!

Brazil has played in every World Cup. They have won five.

Gavin Stokes scored the fastest goal in 2017. It took only 2.1 seconds.

MORE TO EXPLORE

COOL COMPARISONS

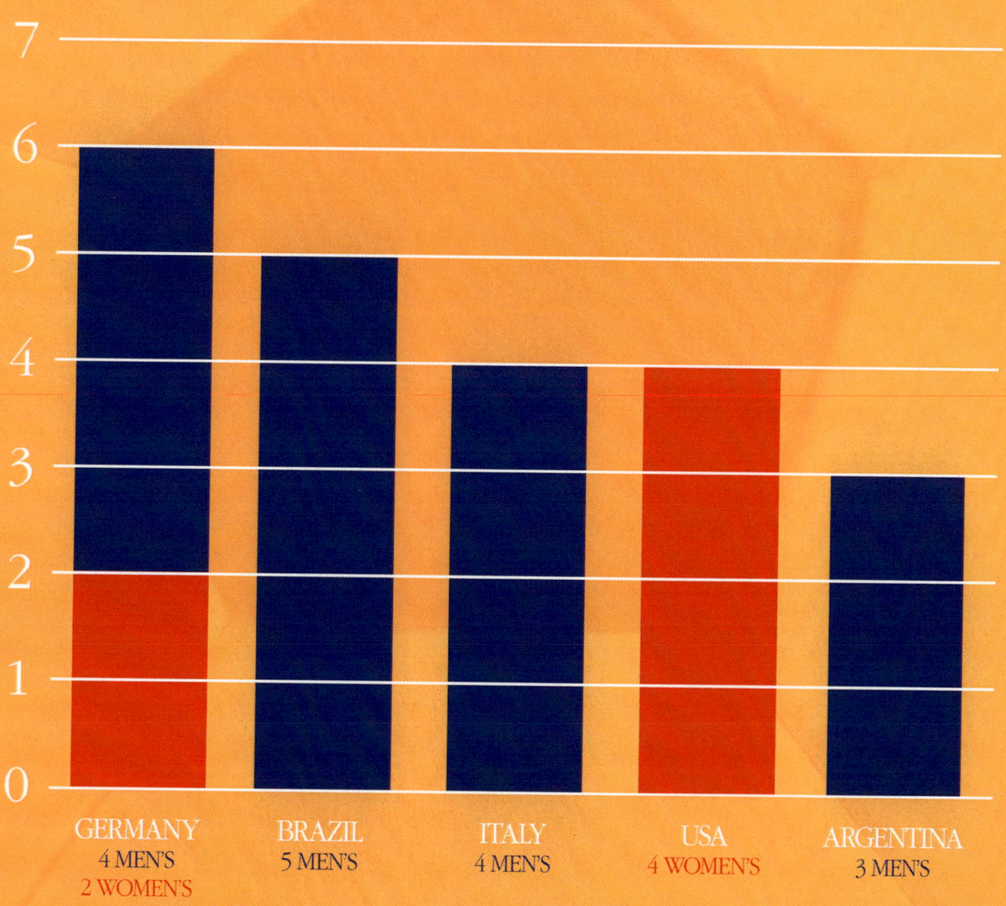

MORE TO EXPLORE

RESOURCES

Glossary

club team (KLUHB TEEM) A group of players that compete in a year-long season.

GOAT A person who is excellent or the best in their field; GOAT stands for "greatest of all time."

league (LEEG) A group of sports teams that play against each other..

national team (NASH-uh-nuhl TEEM) A group of players from the same country that compete against teams from other countries.

tournament (TUR-nuh-muhnt) A series of matches between several teams, ending in one winner.

Read More

Bergland, Bruce. *Soccer GOATs: The Greatest Athletes of All Time*. North Mankato, MN: Capstone Press, 2024.

Tischler, Joe. *Christian Pulisic*. Mankato, MN: Amicus, 2024.

Index

TOP RANK is published by Black Rabbit Books, P.O. Box 227, Mankato, MN, 56002.

• Top Rank is an imprint of Black Rabbit Books. • Designed by Danny Nanos • Photographs © Alamy Stock Photo/Allstar Picture Library, cover, 1; Dreamstime/Dinorah Alejandra Arizpe Valdés, 19; Getty Images/Brad Smith/ISI, 6, Dave Rowland, 4–5, David Ramos – FIFA, 7, Guillermo Legaria, 2 Michael Campanella, 8–9, Shaun Clark, 18; Shutterstock/fifg, 10, Gorodenkoff, cover, 1, grey_and, 12–13, 23, janews, 20, Marco Iacobucci Epp, 14, MDI, 15, NPeter, 12–13, ph.FAB, 21, Photo Works, 16–17, Raffaele Conti 88, 11, Tungphoto, 5

Library of Congress Cataloging-in-Publication Data: Names: Whitcomb, Aidan, author. | Title: Why we love soccer / by Aidan Whitcomb. | Description Mankato, MN : Top Rank is an imprint of Black Rabbit Books, [2026] | Series: Why we love sports | Includes bibliographical references and index. | Ages 8–11 years | Grades 2–3 | Identifiers: LCCN 2024050024 (print) | LCCN 2024050025 (ebook) | ISBN 9781644668078 (lib. bdg.) | ISBN 9781644668399 (paperback) | ISBN 9781644668719 (ebook) | Subjects: LCSH: Soccer—Juvenile literature. | Classification: LCC GV943.25 .W535 2026 (print) | LCC GV943.25 (ebook) | DDC 796.334—dc23/eng/20241211 | LC record available at https://lccn.loc.gov/2024050024